Shying Away From It All!

A Self-Help Guide To
Social Anxiety Disorder

Shying Away From It All!

A Self-Help Guide To
Social Anxiety Disorder

- Are you a shy person, or do you know someone who is? You, or they, may have a disorder known as social anxiety disorder.
- Want help to become more outgoing?
- This book will give you information on social anxiety disorder (social phobia) and offer extremely helpful tips for changing your behaviors and your life.

By: Nicholas J. Hammond BA, MS, PA-C

Aventine Press

Published by Aventine Press
55 E. Emerson St.
Chula Vista CA, 91911

ISBN: 1-59330- 760-8

Table of Contents:

Acknowledgments:

Thanks to my parents for raising me and supporting me throughout my journeys in life. I want to thank the professors at Indiana University in Bloomington for contributing to a superior psychology program, which has assisted me in building a strong educational background. Thanks to all my friends who have stuck with me through thick and thin. Thanks everyone!

Introduction:

If you have always been a shy person or have a hard time doing things in front of others because you feel like you may embarrass yourself, you may actually have a disorder known as social anxiety disorder (SAD). How do you know if you are just shy or actually have this disorder? Being shy or quiet around others is normal. Shyness is a personality characteristic, whereas social anxiety is a psychiatric disorder. People with social anxiety disorder, unlike those who are shy, spend great amounts of time having negative thoughts in anticipation of participating in social activities. After encountering a social event, they replay it in their mind and concentrate on failures or negative moments during the event. It doesn't matter if during the social event everything went well, people with social anxiety disorder imagine they did many things wrong and tend to overexaggerate. They believe that others will see them as stupid or inadequate. Individuals with this disorder have immense anxiety in social situations, which is abnormal. If this describes you, then please read this book for a more in-depth look at this disorder. This book, however, is not a substitute for a professional diagnosis. It will simply give you a better understanding of this disorder and offer some self-help tips. If you have already been diagnosed with social anxiety disorder, you are not alone. Actually, I have been diagnosed with this in the past. I live with it every day and I function as a "normal" person. This is why I want to make the public more aware of this disorder and want to help others in need.

Social anxiety disorder (SAD), also known as social phobia, is the third-most-common psychological disorder in the United States, behind alcoholism and depression. I struggled a great amount of my life with this disorder, mainly because I didn't know it existed. I thought that my shyness was just a personality trait that I would eventually grow out of. However, I never did overcome it and eventually sought out answers to why I acted the way I did in front of others. When I was around familiar people such as my close friends and family, I felt as if I was myself. However, once in the presence of people that I had never met, I was once again that quite, shy guy. I wish I would have been educated about this disorder a long time ago so that I could have received adequate treatment that could have made my life a lot easier. I am hoping that this book will do just that for you. I think you will identify with me and have similar experiences that I have had.

I feel as if it is my calling from God to make the public more aware of this common disorder and help those who suffer with it. I have read many books on social anxiety disorder and have not found one that gave me the answers I was looking for. I didn't feel as if I identified with what the authors were saying. Being a psychotherapist or PhD and reading about a disorder is one thing, but actually living with the disorder and writing to tell about it is another. This book will tell you all you need to know about what social anxiety disorder is, the treatment options you can consider, and the self-help steps you can take to aid yourself in conquering it. I try not only to give pertinent facts but also to provide you with some personal stories of my own past that I am sure you will identify with if you are suffering with this disorder.

There are several points in this book that are very technical and "wordy" at times, so please bear with me. This book is also helpful for parents of children that may exhibit the symptoms of SAD. This can help parents better understand their children and give them treatment options to consider.

I'm originally from Decatur, Indiana, and currently practice medicine as a certified physician assistant in Fort Wayne, Indiana. I received my bachelor's degree with majors in biology, psychology, and a minor in animal behavior at Indiana University in Bloomington. I did my graduate studies at the University of Saint Francis (Fort Wayne, Indiana) and received my master's degree in physician assistant studies. While in school I received a lot of clinical experience in psychiatry and have always had an innate interest in psychology and psychiatric disorders.

Chapter 1:

What is social anxiety disorder?

Social anxiety disorder (SAD), also known as *social phobia*, is a relatively new and overlooked disorder that is prevalent in the United States. If you haven't heard of this disorder before, you are not alone. It has not received much media attention, and therefore many people do not know it exists. SAD was not established as an authentic psychiatric entity until the diagnostic nomenclature of the *American Psychiatric Association DSM III* rendered it an official diagnosis in 1980. People with social anxiety disorder are typically shy, timid, and quiet when around groups of people. They are not comfortable when they are the center of attention. SAD sufferers want the approval and company of others but fear being rejected. They cringe at people seeing them as unlikable or boring. Therefore, they avoid speaking in public, expressing opinions, or even going out with peers; as a result, they are often mistakenly labeled as *snobs*. Many social phobics lack self-esteem, find it difficult to deal with people in authority, and are unable to speak or perform in front of even small groups of people. Exposure to, or anticipation of, the feared social situation leads the individual to either avoid the situation altogether or go through with the event experiencing immense anxiety and discomfort. The individual affected with this disorder usually recognizes that the fear is excessive. Avoidance attempts disrupt the individual's social or occupational functioning. These individuals usually seek out occupations that deal with the least amount of personal contact as possible. Those with SAD usually have few social acquaintances. They understand that their anxiety and fears are not normal but can't seem to overcome these thoughts.

To get a sense of what this disorder is all about and how it presents itself, the following description of a real clinical case of a patient diagnosed with social anxiety disorder is instructive. This patient will be referred to as *Tina*, and she is a 27-year-old supervisor. The following paragraphs are a brief summary of some of her symptoms and the fears she faces on a daily basis. Tina, a supervisor, has been dreading going to work because of the fear that in meetings she will blush, her heart will race, and her thoughts will become so jumbled that she cannot express herself clearly. She is worried about being seen as anxious or uncomfortable. Tina believes that her colleagues will think she is unable to perform at her job because of her anxiety. She has also begun to avoid eating lunch at work based on the fact that she gets very nervous around her coworkers and believes that she will say something embarrassing. Two months ago, Tina received a promotion at work and was anxious about the extra demands being placed upon her. She started using alcohol regularly to relax at the end of the day. Tina had always placed a lot of importance on other people's opinions of her at work, and probably had tended to be overaware of others observing her. Now she was feeling even more self-conscious, particularly in situations involving being challenged by a staff member in front of others. She found meetings quite stressful and had avoided attending on a number of occasions. She did not understand what was happening to her and was considering requesting an extended leave from her employer.

Tina stated that she has always been nervous around authority figures such as teachers in school or higher ups when working at past jobs. She has always found it hard to date and never had a big group of friends growing up. She has a few very close friends whom she confides in and shares everything with. She stated that people around her see her as a serious, quiet, and shy person. Tina has been working with her current company for 3 years, her second job since graduating from college. She said she does not like changing jobs and being in new, unfamiliar situations.

Tina described her mother as a hard-working, stressed person, and her father as fairly strict and a perfectionist. Both parents encouraged her and her younger brother to focus on work and to strive in their respective jobs. This gives you an example of how social anxiety disorder is displayed in a single patient and why it is considered such a disabling disorder.

Social anxiety disorder is the most prevalent of any of the anxiety disorders and is the third-most-common psychiatric disorder following depression and alcohol abuse. Epidemiologic researchers have found that there is a 13.3% lifetime prevalence of social phobia, with a higher rate of occurrences existing in women (15.5%) than in men (11.1%). However, it is estimated that only 2% of the people with social phobia actually seek treatment for it. Many biological, psychological, and social factors are believed to be contributors to the development of social anxiety disorder. There is still a significant amount of research being conducted, and many theories offer explanations of the different contributory factors causing this disorder.

Many research studies have shown that SAD has a genetic link and does tend to run in first-degree relatives. These individuals most likely have abnormalities in the functioning of specific parts of the brain that deal with the anxiety response system. This can be attributed to an improper chemical balance. There are several key neurotransmitters (brain chemicals)— namely serotonin, norepinephrine, and gamma-aminobutyric acid (GABA)—that are produced in the brain and directly affect the way we feel about a given thought or situation. Researchers believe that at least four areas of the brain are critical in playing a role to our anxiety–response system: the brain stem, which regulates cardiovascular and respiratory functions; the limbic system, which regulates mood; the prefrontal cortex, which recognizes risky, dangerous situations; and the motor cortex, which controls our muscular movements. People with SAD are noted to have low levels of the neurotransmitters in the brain, especially serotonin. So, with psychotropic medications, we can manipulate the amount of neurotransmitter levels in the brain. By increasing certain neurotransmitters in the brain, we provide the organ with a sense of emotional well-being.

There are many other theories around how SAD evolves. Many believe that this is a disorder caused through environmental exposure and is a learned behavior. Some researchers believe that an individual develops SAD after experiencing a particular negative social experience in his or her life. After the encounter of the negative event, the individual relates that negative experience to any general social experience he or she encounters in the future. The individual becomes acutely anxious in social situations, fearing that the previous negative social experience will occur again. The result of this is a change in behavior through the avoidance of social situations altogether.

Sometimes, through therapy, people diagnosed with social phobia can recall a specific traumatic incident that sparked their anxiety and irrational thought process. Through my experience, I could specifically nail down one incident from my childhood that ignited my behavior. I was in kindergarten when this occurrence happened. I remembered that I would always get excellent comments on all my work. One day, however, my teacher announced to the class that I actually got something wrong on some sort of project. Many of my classmates made fun of me the rest of the day. This sounds like a very benign event and shouldn't have had such an effect on my life, but it did. The rest of my life I was known as the quiet or shy kid, who never talked. I hated more than anything when someone would say that to me. I will get more into this discussion on how I would deal with this in the chapter with my self-help tips.

Attachment specialists theorize another possible cause of SAD may be an effect of not developing an adequate bond with one's primary caretaker as a child. Researchers state that such children grow up lacking self-regulatory skills to calm, focus, and soothe themselves in situations perceived as stressful or chaotic.

Social anxiety disorder typically begins during childhood with a mean age of onset between 14 and 16 years of age, and is sometimes preceded by a history of social inhibition or shyness in younger years. This is of course just an average age. Social phobia can develop later in life or earlier.

There are two subtypes of social phobia, generalized and circumscribed (nongeneralized). The generalized subtype describes a person who experiences anxiety in numerous situations such as meeting new people, answering questions in class, or interacting socially at all. In Tina's case, she suffered from generalized subtype. The circumscribed subtype is characterized by a fear of acting foolishly in only very specific situations. The most common type of circumscribed social phobia is the fear of public speaking. Don't you remember those people back in school who were terrified when the teacher said that everyone had to do a speech in front of the whole class? For these people, doing a speech in front of others is literally a nightmare. Other commonly feared social situations include fear of trembling when writing in public, fear of choking when eating in public, or being unable to urinate when others are present. Regardless of the subtype, it is not so much the act itself that is feared, but rather the doing of the act in public that arouses the fear. In terms of treatment, the generalized subtype is by far the harder subtype to treat.

When people with SAD approach social situations or sometimes just imagine approaching them, they experience intense anxiety. These individuals often exhibit physical symptoms such as shortness of breath, excessive sweating, tremors, and rapid heartbeat. In some cases, people with this disorder may be able to endure these symptoms and follow through with the situation. In other cases, however, the symptoms are so overwhelming that these individuals may refuse to continue the actions because of their acute fear. In extreme cases, they may even experience a full-blown panic attack.

Individuals with social phobia are often so affected by the disorder that it can complicate many aspects of their life depending on the subtype of the phobia, the patient's occupation, or the social demands placed upon them. For example, an individual with a phobia of public speaking may refuse a promotion for a new position that could involve giving public speeches. Some people with the fear of urinating in public restrooms may choose not to be away from home for long periods. Anxiety and autonomic symptoms may, in fact, impair performance to the point where it is inept. For example, a patient phobic about writing in public may tremble so much that his or her handwriting becomes illegible.

Another serious complication of social phobia is that of alcoholism. Alcohol is commonly utilized in an attempt to decrease anxiety and allow the individual to tolerate the feared social situation. In approximately 85% of the people with both social phobia and alcohol abuse, the social phobia preceded the alcohol problem. Social anxiety makes the treatment of alcoholism more difficult. People with SAD are likely to resist group therapy or self-help meetings such as Alcoholics Anonymous.

I have to admit that I used alcohol in college when placed in social situations. It allowed me to be relaxed around my peers and to open up to them. I felt as if I had no inhibitions and that I could really be like myself around others. This is a dangerous situation, because you then feel like you need to use alcohol whenever you are around others. Pretty soon you will find yourself being dependant on alcohol and having a major problem on your hands. Don't fall into this situation because it is hard to get out of.

Not only is alcoholism a common complication of social phobia, but there are also many comorbid disorders that people may have along with SAD. Depression is one such disorder that is common in persons with SAD. Many believe depression is a secondary effect from SAD and that the social anxiety is the cause of it. There are studies that have found that children with social anxiety have more severe kinds of depression, more relapses, more suicidal ideation, and more suicide attempts than depressed people without the comorbid illness. We can't conclude that social anxiety precedes other illnesses, but we can say it is a predictor of future psychiatric illness.

Tobacco abuse is yet another serious addiction found in concordance with SAD. Kids with social anxiety on average start smoking later than their peers but tend to smoke more and become nicotine dependent more rapidly and more often. As with alcohol, kids may use the nicotine to help relieve anxiety symptoms.

Now that you understand what exactly social anxiety disorder is, I will inform you of how it is diagnosed in the next chapter.

Chapter 2:

How is social anxiety disorder diagnosed?

First, I must give you a word of caution. Reading this chapter does not allow you to diagnose yourself or someone else. Although I am a certified physician assistant, you must visit your family physician or a psychiatrist in order to be accurately diagnosed with social anxiety disorder. The following information will allow you to help recognize symptoms of SAD and the possible need for further diagnostic testing based on the information.

In understanding how serious this disorder is, it is important to recognize the symptoms and—to improve lifestyle—by seeking treatment as soon as possible. *The Diagnostic and Statistical Manual of Mental Disorders*, 4th ed. (DSM-IV), has described social phobia as an intense, irrational, and persistent fear of being scrutinized or negatively evaluated by others. However, to meet the diagnosis for this disorder, the symptoms must be severe enough to cause significant distress or disabilitThe DSM-IV gives a list of diagnostic criteria for social anxiety disorder. The following are the criteria, which according to the DSM-IV must be met for a diagnosis of social phobia. First, there must be a marked and persistent fear of one or more social or performance situation in which the person is exposed to unfamiliar people or to the possibility of scrutiny by others. Second, the person must fear that he or she will act in a way (or show anxiety symptoms) that will be humiliating or embarrassing to himself or herself. In children, there must be evidence of the capacity for age-appropriate social relationships with familiar people, and the anxiety must occur in peer settings, not just in interactions with adults. Third, exposure to the feared social situation almost invariably provokes anxiety, which may take the form of a panic attack. In children, the anxiety may be expressed by crying, tantrums, freezing, or running away from social situations with unfamiliar people. Fourth, the person with SAD must recognize that the fear is excessive or unreasonable. In children, this feature may be absent. Fifth, feared social situations are avoided or else endured with intense anxiety or distress. The avoidance of, anxious anticipation of, or distress in feared social or performance situations must interfere significantly with the person's normal routine, occupational (academic) functioning, social activities, or relationships. In order for individuals under 18 years of age to be diagnosed, the duration of the previous listed symptoms must exist at least 6 months. Sixth, the fear or avoidance cannot be due to the direct physiologic effects of a substance (e.g., drug abuse or a medication) or a general medical condition and is not better accounted for by another mental disorder. In social phobia, fear and avoidance typically develop into a vicious cycle that can become severely distressing, debilitating, and demoralizing over time.

Clinicians can use these guideline criteria for diagnosing social phobia in hopes of effectively treating this condition. Thinking back to the case of Tina, one sees that she displays all of the above criteria that fit the diagnosis of SAD and possibly some signs of alcoholism.

There are many self-tests out there and scales that are used as tools to determine how much difficulty you have in dealing with social situations. The self-tests help you get an idea of how severely social situations affect the way you live. Just another word of caution, you cannot use these scales to diagnose yourself. The rating you get on these scales can help you decide if an experienced clinician might be of use to you in seeking answers. I will supply you with a few scales you can fill out if you wish, and hopefully these will give you a better idea of your level of anxiety.

First published in 2000, the Social Phobia Inventory is a self-rating scale that assesses avoidance, fear, and physiological symptoms. It was originally based off of the Brief Social Phobia Scale. The following is a shortened version of the inventory, which is useful in screening for SAD. This shortened inventory consists of 17 behaviors that the test taker is asked to evaluate on a 5-point scale: 0 = *not at all*, 1 = *a little bit*, 2 = *somewhat*, 3 = *very much*, 4 = *extremely*. The 17 items include the following:

1. I am afraid of people in authority.
2. I am bothered by blushing in front of people.
3. Parties and social events scare me.
4. I avoid talking to people I don't know.
5. Being criticized scares me a lot.
6. Fear of embarrassment causes me to avoid doing things or speaking to people.
7. Sweating in front of people causes me distress.
8. I avoid going to parties.
9. I avoid activities in which I am the center of attention.
10. Talking to strangers scares me.
11. I avoid having to give speeches.
12. I would do anything to avoid being criticized.
13. Heart palpitations bother me when I am around people.
14. I am afraid of doing things when people might be watching.

15. Being embarrassed or looking foolish are among my worst fears.
16. I avoid speaking to anyone in authority.
17. Trembling or shaking in front of others is distressing to me.

After taking this test, add up your points. A score above 19 correlates highly with individuals diagnosed with SAD. In other words, people who have been clinically examined and diagnosed with social anxiety disorder tend to score above 19 on this test.

The second scale I will mention, The Liebowitz Social Anxiety Scale, was developed by M. R. Liebowitz at Columbia University and the New York State Psychiatric Institute. This scale lists 24 social situations in which a patient is asked to rate himself or herself on a scale of 0 to 3 on how much he or she fears the situation and how much he or she tries to avoid the situation. Below is a list of how to rate the following scale and the list of social situations. Fill out each social situation in terms of fear and avoidance.

Fear or Anxiety	Avoidance
0 = *none*	0 = *never* (0%)
1 = *mild*	1 = *occasionally* (1-33%)
2 = *moderate*	2 = *often* (33-67%)
3 = *severe*	3 = *usually* (67-100%)

Now reply to the list of situations below, using one number from each column above.
1. Telephoning in public
2. Participating in small groups
3. Eating in public places
4. Drinking with others in public places
5. Talking to people in authority

6. Acting, performing, or giving a talk in front of an audience
7. Going to a party
8. Working while being observed
9. Writing while being observed
10. Calling someone you don't know very well
11. Talking with people you don't know very well
12. Meeting strangers
13. Urinating in a public bathroom
14. Entering a room when others are already seated
15. Being the center of attention
16. Speaking up at a meeting
17. Taking a test
18. Expressing a disagreement or disapproval to people you don't know very well
19. Looking people you don't know very well in the eyes
20. Giving a report to a group
21. Trying to pick up someone
22. Returning goods to a store
23. Giving a party
24. Resisting a high-pressure salesperson

After giving a score to each situation, add the total score up. Generally speaking, a score of 55-65 indicates moderate social phobia, 65-80 marked social phobia, 80-95 severe social phobia, and greater than 95 very severe social phobia.

Here is The Liebowitz Social Anxiety Scale version adopted for children and adolescents. Use the same rating scale as above and score results.

1. Talking to teachers, other adults
2. Standing up to talk in front of the class
3. Speaking up/raising hand to speak
4. Giving a report in class

5. Calling someone unfamiliar on the telephone
6. Trying to make friends or a date
7. Talking with other unfamiliar children
8. Expressing disagreement to someone not known well
9. Answering the telephone
10. Meeting strangers
11. Being the center of attention
12. Participating in small groups
13. Resisting pressure to join in
14. Looking people in the eyes
15. Going to a party
16. Taking a test
17. Returning something borrowed or bought
18. Entering a room when others are seated
19. Working in class while others are watching
20. Writing in class while others are watching
21. Urinating in a public restroom
22. Having a party
23. Eating in school or restaurants
24. Drinking in school or restaurants

The next scale I will provide you with will help you reveal any strong thought processes you may posses and if some of those thoughts may be irrational in nature. This scale is called, The Social Thoughts and Beliefs Scale and provides some common thoughts of individuals suffering from social phobia. Patients are to rate themselves on 5-point scale (1 = *never*, 2 = *rarely*, 3 = *sometimes*, 4 = *often*, 5 = *always*) to the following statements.

1. When I am in a social situation, I appear clumsy to other people.
2. If I am with a group of people and I have an opinion, I am likely to chicken out and not say what I think.

3. I feel as if other people sound more intelligent than I do.
4. When I am with other people, I am not good at standing up for myself.
5. I am a coward when it comes to interacting with other people.
6. I feel unattractive when I am with other people.
7. I would never be able to make a good speech in public.
8. Other people are more comfortable in social situations than I am.
9. Other people are more socially capable than I am.
10. No matter what I do, I will always be uncomfortable in social situations.
11. My mind is very likely to go blank when I am talking in a social situation.
12. I am not good at making small talk.
13. Other people are bored when they are around me.
14. When speaking in a group, others will think what I am saying is stupid.
15. If I am around someone I am interested in, I am likely to get panicky or do something to embarrass myself.
16. I do not know how to behave when I am in the company of others.
17. If something went wrong in a social situation, I would not be able to smooth it over.
18. When I am with other people, they usually don't think I am very smart.
19. When other people laugh, it feels as if they are laughing at me.
20. People can easily see when I am nervous.
21. If there is a pause during a conversion, I feel as if I have done something wrong.

Add up your ratings. The mean score for people with SAD is 52, and for people who don't suffer from SAD have a mean score of 22.

The last scale I want to give you is called The Brief Social Phobia Scale, and was adapted by J. R. Davidson. This is different from the previous scales because it is an observer-rated scale. Also, it is for people who have already been diagnosed with social phobia and are measuring how much improvement they have made with treatment. Here someone poses questions to an individual and reports their reactions. This includes three subscales: fear, avoidance, and physiological arousal symptoms. The observer would ask the following questions to a patient and rate them on a 5-point scale, with 1 being least feared or avoided. The mean score with those diagnosed with social phobia is 42.

1. How much do you fear:
   Speaking in public
   Talking to people in authority
   Talking to strangers
   Being embarrassed or humiliated
   Being criticized
   Social gatherings
   Doing something while being watched
2. How much do you avoid:
   Speaking in public
   Talking to people in authority
   Talking to strangers
   Being embarrassed or humiliated
   Being criticized
   Social gatherings
   Doing something while being watched
3. How much do you feel these symptoms in contemplating social interactions (1 to 5 scale, least to most):
   Blushing

Palpitations
Tremors
Sweating

You can use these self-tests for yourself or someone you believe may have a social phobia. Just please remember that these tests are not a substitute for a diagnosis from a trained clinician.

Chapter 3:

Treatment options

Many individuals who have social anxiety disorder do not seek treatment. Those who do choose to change their lives and actively seek treatment have several options offered to them. The first topic that will be discussed is also the most popular means of treatment, this being drug therapy. It is used most commonly because it gives quick and moderately successful results. Effective types of drugs used to treat SAD include selective serotonin reuptake inhibitors (SSRIs), monoamine oxidase inhibitors (MAOIs), benzodiazepines, and beta blockers (blood pressure medication). Although drug therapy is successful in relieving many people's anxiety, they still exhibit the continued irrational thought process in social situations. The second topic discussed will be psychotherapy, which has been shown in some studies to offer individuals long-term successful results because it addresses their maladaptive thought processes and works towards restructuring their thought processes. Psychotherapy is usually offered through individual consultations with a psychotherapist or in a group setting led by a therapist.

Before initiating pharmacotherapy, a physician must first diagnose the patient as having generalized subtype or circumscribed subtype, because they are each treated differently. Patients with generalized subtype of social phobia respond best to daily scheduled drug dosages, typically antidepressants, which they will more than likely be on for the rest of their lives. On the other hand, patients with the circumscribed subtype usually are started on a beta blocker (blood pressure lowering medication) that is taken an hour before being exposed to the anticipated feared situation. I will describe later in the next chapter how a blood pressure lowering medication works to lower anxiety.

With regard to the generalized subtype, various drugs are available, including selective serotonin reuptake inhibitors (SSRIs), monoamine oxidase inhibitors (MAOIs), and benzodiazepines. Among the SSRIs, Zoloft, Paxil, and fluovoxamine have all been shown to be effective in several research studies. Fluoxetine (Prozac), however, has had mixed results in a number of studies and seems not to be as effective as other SSRIs. Clonazepam, a benzodiazepine, is also effective in treatment, but patients tend to build up tolerance to the drug and it must be tapered slowly to avoid withdrawal anxiety. Of the MAOIs, phenelzine has been found to have high response rates and brofaromine, a reversible MAOI not available in the United States, is also effective. Choosing among these various options is difficult, in large part because there are not many studies comparing drugs directly. The SSRIs are all easy to use and generally well tolerated. Given that the SSRIs have the most experimental backing and the least number of side effects, it is reasonable to begin with one of these.

With regard to the circumscribed subtype, patients troubled by prominent autonomic symptoms (e.g., tremor or rapid heart rate) may be treated with propranolol (beta-blocker) on an as needed basis about an hour before encountering the social situation. In cases where the social situation will outlast the half-life of immediate-release propranolol, a long-acting preparation may be used.

Aside from drug therapy treatment in SAD, numerous studies have demonstrated the efficacy of psychological treatments for social phobia, especially two specific therapies known as cognitive-behavioral therapy and exposure therapy. The most widely investigated psychotherapy treatment approach for SAD is cognitive-behavioral therapy. Cognitive-behavioral therapy (CBT) combines treatment approaches of both cognitive and behavioral therapies. The principles were first outlined in a treatment manual specifically targeted to depression by Beck et al. (year).

The basis of cognitive therapy is the observation that negative feelings result from faulty ways of processing information in the brain. Incoming information is selectively filtered so that perceptions are distorted toward negative conclusions. By examining a patient's spontaneous thoughts and actions throughout the day, the specific faulty processing can be identified. These "automatic" thoughts are the keys to understanding a patient's core system of assumptions and beliefs about the self and surroundings. Many patients can recall a past event in their lives that most likely resulted in their present core beliefs. The therapist can help the patient trace how their core schemas may have evolved from painful early experiences. CBT treatments first help a patient become aware of faulty automatic thoughts and underlying assumptions. It then allows modification of their beliefs on a more balanced view of all available information. Throughout the CBT treatment program, behavioral techniques are integrated to facilitate change. Specific exercises for thought stopping, relaxation, and impulse control may be combined with monitoring and adjusting daily activities to increase mastery and pleasure experiences. Graded task assignments and desensitization through exposure exercises (which will be discussed later) may also be used to help patients develop new coping skills and ways of seeing things in a new, positive light.

Group CBT also is helpful in the treatment of social phobia. This form of treatment includes (a) training in cognitive coping skills, (b) multiple exposures to simulations of feared situations in session, (c) homework assignments for exposure to feared situations, (d) use of cognitive coping skills in conjunction with exposures, and (e) direct, immediate feedback on their perceptions of how others view them. Basically group CBT is similar to regular CBT but adds the element of being in a group with others having similar problems. The group therapy gives you a sense that you are not alone and that others struggle with similar problems. It allows several participants to simulate social situations in a controlled atmosphere with each other before they go out in real public situations. Cognitive behavioral group therapy has been evaluated in several studies and has shown to be effective in the long term.

Another effective psychotherapy for social phobia is exposure therapy. It is often part of cognitive-behavioral treatment programs for phobias. Exposure therapy is a process in which the phobic person is exposed to the feared situations or objects. The theory behind exposure therapy is basic: through exposure, the phobic person comes to see that the situation or object will not cause harm. There are two different specific types of exposure therapy, systematic desensitization and intensive exposure. Systematic desensitization is like a ladder in that patients are slowly exposed to more and more fearful exposure situations. In time, patients learn that the social situation they feared becomes easier to face. Intensive exposure therapy, also called *flooding*, is the rapid exposure to feared situations. Patients are thrown into the situation they fear, right off the bat. By throwing patients into such a situation, they are shown that they can make it through the thing they fear without it harming them, even though they may experience intense anxiety. Exposure has also been shown to be extremely effective for individuals diagnosed with nongeneralized social anxiety disorder. For example, those who have a phobia of doing speeches in front of others can practice by doing speeches many times in front of public audiences until their anxiety is lowered to a tolerable level.

Now that I have given you a basic general idea of what cognitive therapy entails, I will delve into a much deeper look at this therapy in the next chapter. The next chapter is an important chapter to pay attention to so you understand why you will be doing the specific exercises you will be doing.

Chapter 4:

Understanding the basis of cognitive therapy

In this chapter, I want to give you an overview of cognitive therapy and how it helps to change your perceptions that have a negative affect on your feelings and actions. Cognitive therapy is based on a few key principles. The first principle is that how you look at different circumstances directly affects your mood. The second principle goes along with the first in that; if you change your viewpoint on things, this directly will change your mood and outlook. The third principle is working on how to improve your thoughts and beliefs. Cognitive therapy is directed at changing your thought process in order to improve your feeling of wellness. It works by changing your negative thought processing into new ways of thinking and viewing incoming information.

Say that you and a friend visit a city such as Seattle, Washington. You both hang out together and do the same activities while visiting. When you get back from your trip, someone comes up to the both of you and asks how your trip was. Your friend talks about how much fun the city was and how there was so much to do. You on the other hand, dwell on the fact that it rained every other day and don't mention anything about the activities you both did. It's like seeing the glass as half full or half empty. Each of us develops his or her own personal view of an event or experience. This experience is filtered and interpreted in our own unique ways. We all use our own points of view as a basis for forming our opinions and conclusions. Our own ways of seeing things become habitual, and we forget that there are other points of view. It is almost as if our minds are machines and we only process information in one type of perspective that we were programmed with, whereas another person may see the same image or go through the same situation and process it in a different way. The point that I am making is that there is always more than one way to see something. People who have SAD have a set negative ways of seeing social situations. Before even walking into a social situation, they have a preprocessed negative attitude. No matter what may happen in some sort of social event, a person with SAD automatically thinks of himself or herself looking foolish in front of others. This preprocessed way of seeing social events leads the person to fear social situations of every type. Fear is what guides these individuals to avoid interacting with people in every possible way. This is a vicious cycle that social phobics fall into, making it such a devastating disorder that is difficult to treat. The key is to try and change these individuals' ways of thinking and seeing things. This is, however, difficult, knowing that you have been processing information the same way for years and years. It's like going into the gym one day and your coach tries to change the way you shoot a basketball. You have been using the same technique for years, and he tells you to change your grip on the ball. At first this may be totally awkward to you, but with repetition you will get better at the different technique.

To enable yourself to change, you must first recognize your negative thinking and then attempt to consciously change your way of thinking. Those with SAD have several incorrect views in common that will be addressed. The first incorrect and negative way of thinking is predicting the worst outcome before the social situation occurs. You believe that if this event goes wrong it will be a disaster. The second most common misconception in individuals with SAD is that of overgeneralizing situations. This is when one assumes that because something negative happened once in the past, it will always happen. Many people, on the other hand, could come to the conclusion that one negative event may just be by chance and they would never have a second thought in a similar situation in the future. Another quality exhibited by those with social phobia is that they exaggerate negative events. They give negative events more importance than they really deserve, and positive events less importance. These patients discount positive events in that they believe when something good does come out of a social event, it is merely luck. Those with social anxiety also do what is known as *mind reading*. This means that they believe they can predict what another individual thinks of them. For example, after a brief conversation, persons with social anxiety may automatically believe their acquaintance thought of them as uneducated and not worthy of talking to again. Individuals with SAD take almost everything personally. This was true with myself. If someone would try to give me constructive criticism, I would automatically take it personally and think he or she was directly attacking me. Another common characteristic of those with social phobia is that they seem to always blame themselves for many things, while constantly calling themselves names on the inside. They question themselves about things they could have done differently.

In chapter 7, I will give you specific instructions on how you can help yourself recreate the way you think. After improving your way of thinking, the second step in therapy is actually facing your fears.

Behavioral therapy is used in helping you actually face your challenges and overcome them. Exposure therapy is a very useful and an important step used in behavioral therapy aiding in overcoming social fears. In chapter 8, I will go through steps that you can follow to actually go out into the world and practice your skills.

Chapter 5:

Do you have more questions or concerns about taking psychotropic medications? Pro's and con's to consider before starting medications for SAD

Many individuals do have reservations about starting psychotropic medications. They think they are weak or will become dependent if they start taking medications for psychological disorders. This is far from the truth. Medications these days are becoming more accepted and have far fewer side effects than in years past.

The following is a description of each of the previously mentioned classes of anti-anxiety medications and the pros and cons of each class.

Monoamine Oxidase Inhibitors

The monoamine oxidase inhibitors (MAOIs) have performed well in clinical trials for treatment of generalized social phobia. Phenelzine (Nardil) in particular has been tested extensively in placebo-controlled studies. Open and controlled trials suggest that approximately two thirds of patients will show clinically significant improvement during acute treatment with these agents.

For treatment of social phobia, MAOIs are usually not the first line of agents used because of strict diet restrictions and adverse effects associated with them. MAO is an enzyme found in the liver, intestinal wall, and neurons. MAO in neurons functions to convert monoamine neurotransmitters; norepinephrine (NE), serotonin, and dopamine, into inactive products. In the liver and intestine, MAO inactivates tyramine and other biogenic amines in food. MAOIs therefore inhibit these enzymes. In neurons, MAOIs inhibit intraneuronal MAO, which in turn increases the amount of norepinephrine (NE), serotonin, and dopamine available for release. These drugs therefore intensify transmission at junction sites. The neurotransmitters: NE, serotonin, and dopamine, function in the brain to give you a sense of well-being.

The MAOIs do, however, have restrictions and adverse risks that should be considered during treatment planning. MAOIs require users to partake in a low-tyramine diet, which prohibits the partaking in many popular foods such as cheese products and wine. These dietary restrictions will deter some patients from accepting therapy with MAOIs. Patients risk a potentially fatal hypertensive reaction if they do not comply with the diet. Common adverse effects at therapeutic dosages include postural hypotension, sedation, sexual dysfunction, and weight gain. Some common over-the-counter medications, such as cold and cough remedies, are contraindicated in patients using MAOIs. Reversible MAOIs such as moclobemide, which do not require dietary restrictions, showed promise in early trials.

Although their advantages have led many to consider MAOIs an appropriate first-line treatments, their disadvantages have prompted others to relegate them to a second-line position behind the newer innovations in antidepressants.

Selective Serotonin Reuptake Inhibitors

Several studies have supported the efficacy of selective serotonin reuptake inhibitors (SSRIs), including large controlled trials of paroxetine (Paxil) and fluvoxamine (Luvox); smaller controlled trials of sertraline (Zoloft); and most recently, an open, uncontrolled trial of citalopram (Celexa). SSRIs are usually the first-line treatment in social phobia and have been thoroughly studied in research trials. SSRIs produce selective inhibition of serotonin reuptake, thereby intensifying transmission at serotonergic synapses. The blockade of serotonin uptake occurs quickly, whereas therapeutic effects develop slowly. The delay suggests that therapeutic effects are the result of adaptive cellular changes that take place in response to prolonged uptake blockades. As a group, SSRIs have shown acute-treatment improvement rates ranging from 50% to 75% of patients. SSRIs are currently considered an appropriate first-line treatment because they are relatively safe and tolerable. SSRIs have a low side effect profile and are nonhabit forming. They also do not require dietary restrictions as MAOIs do. I recommend starting patients on an SSRI as a first line drug therapy. I have also taken an SSRI in the past for social anxiety disorder, and it helped me significantly with anxiety levels. I also did not have any side effects taking this medication, which was definitely a positive.

Benzodiazepines

Another option for treating SAD is the usage of benzodiazepines (anti-anxiety medication). Controlled studies of alprazolam (Xanax) and clonazepam (Klonopin) report acute-treatment improvement rates ranging from approximately 40% to 80%, with clonazepam showing more favorable results. These are fast-acting, well-tolerated anxiolytics that have shown efficacy in acute treatment. Benzodiazepines potentiate the actions of gamma-aminobutyric acid (GABA), an inhibitory neurotransmitter found throughout the central nervous system. These drugs enhance the actions of GABA by binding to specific receptors in a supramolecular structure known as the GABA receptor-chloride channel complex and induce the flow of chloride ions into the molecule. The influx of chloride ions hyperpolarizes the neuron and thereby decreases the cell's ability to fire. Benzodiazepines do have drawbacks of being habit forming. Standing dosages are sometimes difficult for patients to taper and discontinue without symptomatic worsening and a high risk of acute relapse.

Benzodiazepines must be used with caution in patients with a history of substance abuse because of their ability to produce physical dependence. When these drugs are used as needed in performance-related situations, sedation, and psychological reliance can develop. Given those risks, benzodiazepines are considered for use in patients with a low risk for substance abuse and those unresponsive to alternative treatments such as SSRIs and MAO inhibitors. The most common use of these agents, however, is in low-dose therapy for initial-symptom relief in conjunction with an antidepressant, psychotherapy, or both. I would recommend this to a patient that has nongeneralized SAD and who has had no response to the use of a beta blocker. These patients would use the benzodiazepine only prior to the feared social situation on an as-needed basis. This would prevent tolerance to this drug and hinder patients from abuse.

Beta-Adrenergic Blockers
Treatment studies of beta blockers for social phobia display mixed results. Controlled trials using standing dosages for generalized social phobia have been discouraging. Prominent symptoms of the circumscribed type of social phobia include tachycardia and sweating brought on by generalized discharge of the sympathetic nervous system. Beta blockers such as propranolol (Inderal) appear to be clinically effective when used in low doses on an as-needed basis for mild to moderate circumscribed performance anxiety. Beta blockers help by preventing beta 1-mediated tachycardia (fast heart rate). They specifically reduce heart rate, reduce force of contraction,

and reduce the velocity of impulse conduction through the heart. These drugs should be used only intermittently until the patient's confidence in performance situations is restored. Although beta blockers have been shown to be effective in the treatment of circumscribed social phobia, beta blockers lack significant positive results of change in generalized social phobia. Contraindications for beta blocker use include asthma, sinus bradycardia (slow heart rate), greater than first-degree heart block, cardiogenic shock, and some cases of congestive heart failure.

There are many studies in the works to help show how effective these different types of medications are in treating this disorder. Remember to also talk with your doctor regarding these different classes of medicines and the possible side effects.

Chapter 6:

Changing your pattern of thinking and learning relaxation techniques.

This chapter will give you the basic skills and understanding you will need in starting your journey to recovery. Before changing your behaviors, you must change your mind set through the way you think and process information. It is important to master basic skills before moving on to tougher and larger goals. These next couple of chapters will give you a guide to follow in planning your journey.

Before I go into how you can change the negative way you process your thoughts, I would like to give you some relaxation techniques. I believe the key to starting recovery is to first be able to control your physical self before you can work on the mental part. Anxiety can be relieved in many ways. Please sit down and try some of these relaxation techniques that I will provide you. If one technique seems to work better than another, then stay with the one that helps you. Practice your relaxation techniques daily and get in a habit of setting aside time each day for this. I believe if you master some of these techniques they will help you out significantly when it comes to actually going out in a social environment and facing your fears.

One of the easiest ways to release some anxiety is by doing deep breathing exercises that will allow you to relax around others. This involves taking a deep breath and releasing it very slowly. You can take a deep breath and then release it to a count of three or four. This will take all that stress inside you and make you feel as if you are releasing it out of your body. You can use this technique even in the presence of other people, but it is best to practice it first when you are alone. This is only one of many relaxation techniques you can do. If you want some more help with this, you can purchase information tapes on techniques.

An additional relaxation technique that may seem cheesy but has been shown to be effective is that of visualization. Visualization is done by picturing a social situation in your mind prior to the experience you wish to have. For example, picture yourself giving a speech in front of others and delivering the information perfectly. The audience looks at you in great interest and even applauds after you are finished. If you do this often, it is very effective.

Another visualization strategy is to sit quietly and imagine yourself going someplace that you find especially relaxing. Imagine all of the sights, sounds, smells, and so on of this place while taking deep breaths and relaxing the tense muscles of your body. You can use this technique before meeting new people, going out on dates, attending meetings, or any situation that typically causes you to feel anxious.

Muscle relaxation exercises are very effective in reducing stress. This involves tensing and relaxing multiple muscle groups. Through tensing each muscle you will recognize when your body is under tension. You will learn to identify certain muscle groups that give you the most tension when you are under stress. By identifying what muscles groups give you the most trouble, you can learn to do relaxation exercises before you come into a situation in which you experience anxiety.

Before you start the muscle relaxation exercises, find a quiet place with plenty of room to spread out. You can start by either sitting or lying down. The overall outline for each muscle group is to start with a deep breath in, using your abdominal muscles and a breath out, through your mouth. Next, separately tense each muscle group, holding tension for five to ten seconds, Next, release the tension slowly. Then take another slow deep breath in and out. With this outline in mind, I will cover each of the most important muscle groups and tell you what to tense and what to relax.

Head
1) Close your eyes tightly and hold.
2) Open your eyes as wide as possible.
3) Next clinch your jaw and bite down.
4) Relax your jaw and all of your teeth.
5) Make a big smile and hold.
6) Relax your face.

Torso and shoulders
1) Press your chin to your chest, hold and then relax.
2) Then tilt your head toward your back, hold, and then relax.
3) Tilt your head to your left shoulder, hold, and then relax.
4) Tilt your head to your right shoulder, hold, and then relax.
5) Raise both of your shoulders upward, hold, and then relax.

Chest
1) Take a deep breath and make your chest barrel out, hold, and then relax.
2) Tighten your chest muscle along with your pectorals, hold, and then relax.

Back
1) Bend down and touch your toes, hold, and then come back to a standing position.
2) Bend your upper body to the right, hold, relax, and then to the left, hold, and relax.

    3) Twist your upper torso to the right, hold, and relax, and then to the left, hold, and relax.

Abdomen

    1) Flex your abdominal muscles while bending forward in a sitting position, hold, and relax.

    2) Push your abdomen out as far as you can, hold, and relax.

Arms and Hands

    1) Made two fists and squeeze, hold, and relax.

    2) Flex your biceps and triceps, hold, and relax.

    3) Push on a wall with some force, hold, and relax.

Hips, Legs, and Feet

    1) Tighten your buttocks, hold, and relax.

    2) Stand on the back of your feet, hold. and relax.

    3) Point your toes upward in the air, hold. and relax.

    4) Point your toes downward toward the ground, hold, and relax.

These are the main muscle groups to concentrate on. If you have problems with a specific muscle group, then skip it. Many people have pinched nerves and spinal problems, so it would be a good idea to skip the neck and back exercises.

Now that you have learned some relaxation techniques, you can now concentrate on changing your pattern of thinking. Before you learn how to change the pattern of your thinking, you must identify your current maladaptive thoughts and how they affect how you view social situations. All people have an ongoing stream of thoughts that runs through their heads and just pops up without any effort. Psychologists call these thoughts *automatic thoughts*. These thoughts are automatic reactions to whatever situation you happen to be in. People with SAD share a similar set of automatic thoughts that are maladaptive. Let me give you an example of this sort of situation. Say you have to go to a dinner meeting to meet a new employee. You sit down with him or her and have dinner with much conversation during the evening. After the dinner is over and you are heading home, you have the following thoughts running through your head. "Oh, I sounded so stupid tonight. How will I ever work with this person after they have met me? They are probably thinking how in the world I got the job I did if I am so dumb. This situation becomes a trigger for these sorts of maladaptive thoughts. The thoughts are so distracting that you may end up failing because you believe your maladaptive thoughts to the fullest.

Individuals with social phobia have a number of unrealistic beliefs that cause them to think maladaptively in social situations. These unrealistic beliefs are carried with them everywhere and are used as general principles about situations, people, and themself. Many people don't even realize they have these automatic beliefs and ways of viewing things. One such belief that I used to have with my disorder is the following: Whenever I was criticized for one specific thing that I did, I believed that it was an attack on my overall worth as a person. Another belief of mine was that if someone found out that I wasn't as talkative as everyone else, then I would be labeled as weird and stuck up. You need to sit down and actually brainstorm what goes through your head in certain events. Write all the general beliefs you have down on a piece of paper so you can revert back to them when trying to adjust your thinking process. I will supply you with some blank pages in the book to write down some notes and brainstorm.

Many of the unrealistic beliefs people have with social phobia tend to contain the idea that they must avoid the disapproval of others. The other concept that many of these individuals have is the fact they are perfectionists. They believe that they cannot make a mistake in front of another person or they will get disapproval. This is obviously an impossible goal to attain, and individuals with social phobia will never overcome their disorder until their belief in perfectionism changes.

Another common characteristic of people with social anxiety is that they believe they have to be liked and gain the approval of everyone around them. You must understand that not everyone in the world will be fond of you. If you judge yourself by what others think, you will lose. Folks with SAD exaggerate the chances of disapproval occurring and the consequences if disapproval does occur. They expect disapproval in almost every social event even when it is very unlikely. People with this disorder must come to terms that it is okay not to have the approval of everyone all of the time.

The first step in recovery is to identify your maladaptive thoughts. Buy a little notebook to start off. You can quickly come to realize what your maladaptive thoughts are by keeping a written record of them on a daily basis. I will also leave you space in this book to write some notes for yourself. After you have encountered a social situation, record an uncensored version of your thoughts that had run through your mind in that situation. An example of something that you might write down includes the following: "Wow, I really must be looking stupid to this new person I met; they will never want to talk to me again. They probably think that I'm a quiet, weird person." Just write down everything that you are thinking inside.

Describe on event: Your unrealistic beliefs to the event:

_____

_____

_____

_____

_____

_____

_____

_____

_____

_____

_____

_____

_____

_____

_____

_____

_____

_____

_____

_____

_____

_____

_____

_____

_____

_____

_____

_____

_____

_____

After you have made a laundry list and a good effort at monitoring and recording your thoughts, you now have an idea of what thoughts go through your mind in a feared social situation. It is now time to determine what unrealistic beliefs you have. The beliefs you may have are not always that obvious and you may not be consciously aware of them. In my thought diary I had entries that talked about moments in school. There were several entries where someone had corrected me in class and I believed that the person correcting me thought I was completely stupid. I believed that they would never want help from me in the future, based on one mistake that I made. The overall unrealistic belief I had come up with was that if I was criticized for one specific mistake, it was a criticism of my overall knowledge base and worth as a person. This was a major belief that I had to overcome in treating my SAD.

So, with this example in mind, go through your lists of thoughts and find some unrealistic beliefs you may have. Read over your beliefs and make it evident to yourself why these beliefs are incorrect and unrealistic.

List your Maladaptive Thoughts here:

_____

_____

_____

_____

_____

_____

_____

_____

_____

_____

_____

_____

_____

_____

_____

_____

_____

_____

_____

_____

_____

_____

_____

_____

_____

_____

_____

_____

_____

_____

_____

By identifying your maladaptive thoughts you can now learn to replace these with constructive thoughts found in coping statements. Coping statements are statements that you make up yourself to substitute for the maladaptive thoughts in your mind. I will give you some examples of coping statements, but first some tips on making them. First, I would memorize them if I were you, so make your statements short and simple. Make sure that the statement you make is realistic and positive. Don't make a statement that has negative words such as *can't*, *will not*, *never*, and so on. You need to make coping statements that apply to your direct concerns in public situations. If you worry about making eye contact with a person, then make a coping statement that directly addresses that problem you have.

Look back at your list of maladaptive thoughts. Start writing coping statements for each of those thoughts. A general outline follows: "Most people will accept my actions if (what you fear occurs). I can cope with disapproval. It is not that big of deal." The first sentence should remind you that the chance of disapproval is lower than what your fear says it is. The second sentence tells you that you can deal with disapproval if it may occur and that the consequences of disapproval are not as severe as your fear tries to make you believe it will be. The following is a personal coping statement of mine that I wrote in the past: "If I may make a mistake in front of someone, that person will most likely not judge my overall character based on a minor mistake I have made. If they do, then it is their loss for not getting to know me. I can cope with disapproval, and it is not a big deal."

Maladaptive Thought: Coping Statement to each Maladaptive Though:

After you have written your coping statements, it is time to put them to use. First, memorize your statements. Second, repeat your statements to yourself when you begin to feel anxious. By repeating your coping statements to yourself, you will interrupt the maladaptive thoughts going through your head. You should practice saying your coping statements daily so you can retrieve them from your brain instantly when you need to use them. Although coping statements are good in that they interrupt your maladaptive thoughts, you must go one step further to have a lasting recovery.

That next step on the ladder is adopting more accurate expectations when it comes to social situations you will be in. I believe a great exercise to do here is to gather up some of your close friends or family members whom you trust and who do not have social fears of their own. Sit down with them and describe to them a social situation in which you fear and the consequences that you feel may come of this. For example, if I am talking with someone new and my face starts to turn red, I believe that the person will think that I'm weird and will not want to talk to me again. Ask your friend to play the part of that new person you are talking to. Ask him or her what he or she would think of you or if he or she would disapprove of you in that situation. Just get a feeling of what is going through their head and compare it with your own internal thoughts. After you have gotten a sense of how others process similar situations, go back and reanalyze your expectations in feared social situations. Do you believe maybe you are over-exaggerating the chance of disapproval? Do you think that maybe others do not process similar situations the way you do? Go over each feared situation you have written down in the past and write down why you believe that your thought process was unreasonable at that time.

The last step on your road to recovery is actually changing your beliefs. This takes time. You must understand that changing your beliefs will not be as fast as changing your thoughts and expectations. You will have to work very hard. The most influential way in which to change your beliefs is through a technique that I will walk you through in the next chapter. This technique is called exposure, and it directly tests whether your beliefs and expectations are accurate.

Chapter 7:

A self-help guide to recovering from social anxiety disorder

This part of the book is about taking everything you learned in preparation to recovering from SAD and putting it into action. Changing your beliefs is key to this chapter. I also added some additional key topics such as, how to improve your presentation skills and a self-help guide you can follow. I am in no way a psychotherapist, and this chapter of the book is in no way a cure-all solution. This information may help some, but you may need additional help. Please consider consulting your own professional therapist in adequately giving you the tools you need to succeed. I believe that these ideas I will present to you will at the least give some individuals the confidence they need in overcoming their disorder. Overcoming or lessening your fear of social situations takes time. My tip to you is to be persistent yet patient.

First off, I just want to start by saying if you have an alcohol or drug addiction, you must take care of this first before you can directly deal with SAD. Alcohol or drug addiction is very commonly associated with SAD, and you must seek treatment for this before it overtakes you. There are many skilled rehabilitation facilities that have been successful helping with these sorts of problems. I know it must sound scary for you to actually go through drug or alcohol rehab, but these treatment facilities are confidential, and you can get help without anyone knowing you did. If you are working, just tell your employer you must take a leave of absence due to personal issues so you do not have discuss the fact that you may have a drug or alcohol problem. This is perfectly legal, and you never have to disclose what the personal matter entails. There are also outpatient alcohol and drug programs available. There is no way to fully recover from SAD without first conquering your alcohol or drug addiction. Now that I got that out in the open, we can continue talking about treatment for SAD.

You may remember that in cognitive-behavioral therapy for treating SAD, exposure is a great amount of what the behavior section is made up of. So this topic will make up most of this chapter. Exposure is basically facing your fears instead of avoiding them at all costs. It works by allowing you to learn that certain actions will not lead to disapproval by others, and if disapproval does occur, it is not the end of the world. After repeated exposures, you will be desensitized to anxiety-provoking situations. You will find yourself being calmer in situations that in the past made you anxious. Remember, exposure therapy is executed in a step-wise order. You start out with less-anxiety-provoking situations and work your way up to situations that bring you a great deal of fear. By taking this step-wise approach, you build confidence each time you conquer another feared situation.

Before starting behavioral therapy and going through exposures, you must be very motivated. It is like smoking: If you don't really want to stop smoking, you will not quit, no matter if you are on medication or in therapy. You must believe that if you go through all of this that it will pay off in the end. Your life will be so much better and you will have a sense of relief. Many people, once they have gone through an exposure, are surprised that the situation they had feared for so long was really not that bad. Most of the exposures you will go through will bring you anxiety, but this will be the only way you will learn how to cope with it. Eventually you will gain more self-esteem and be more in control when presented with these situations. This will allow you to become less fearful and more comfortable in social situations.

There are really two types of exposure therapy. The first type is called *imaginal exposure therapy*. This is the exposure therapy I will introduce to you first. It consists of actually sitting down and going over a social interaction you fear in your mind. While in this state of mind you visualize your surroundings: the smells, sounds, and everything in your environment to make it as real as possible. During this time, you actually go through your relaxation exercises and imagine what you would say or do in that sort of social situation. Imaginal exposure therapy is a precursor that helps to prepare you for what is known as *in vivo exposure*. In vivo exposure is the real-life thing. You actually go out and seek real-life social situations. Say, for example, you are terrified of snakes. Maybe you would start with looking at pictures of snakes in books, then visualizing holding a snake. You then could watch someone actually holding a snake and realize it is not hurting the person. Last, after all of these precursor steps, you could finally sit and expose yourself to holding a snake. It is the baby steps leading up to the ultimate feared exposure that calm your anxiety and begin to make you more comfortable in reaching your goal.

The first step before initiating exposure therapy is to make a list of situations you associate with fear or disapproval. Sit down and make a detailed list of specifically what situations you fear and want to learn to be less anxious over. Go into detail for each situation, listing how each makes you feel and the exact details of how you act in each situation. One personal example that I used follows: I am very anxious when I have to go out to dinner with new business partners. What I did in attempting to deal with this situation was to first sit down and list everything that I feared about this situation. I feared that the individual I was having dinner with would label me as quiet and weird for not talking much. I was worried about having pauses in conversation and not having anything to talk about. I feared that the person would not like me and would believe that I did not like him or her because I would not talk much. I would be worried about doing something embarrassing during dinner, such as spilling a drink on myself or getting food on my clothes. I will give you some paper space to write down some of your ideas.

Situations You Fear: How you Feel in Each Situation:

The next step was to make objectives I would like to obtain for this specific situation. First, I wanted to go to dinner with a certain list of conversation items I could bring up with my business partner. I wanted to make a list of things that I could tell the individual about myself that might make that person more comfortable with me. I wanted to prepare a list of questions I could ask about my cohort. I desired to be able to feel as if I could speak freely without the idea that I would say something stupid. I wanted to sit through a whole dinner without spilling something on myself so that I could give myself the confidence that I can make it through dinner without doing something embarrassing.

Below I have provided space to write a list of your own objectives.

Specific Situation: Objectives you have for each situation:

After writing a list of the feared situations you would like help with, you can now plan what exposures you would like to do. For example, some people are just fearful of any social contact whatsoever. These individuals may have a general of exposures they would like to start off with. To help you out, if you are one that is fearful of social interaction at all, then I would follow a similar list to the following one:

- Visit a nursing home and talk to some of the residents there. They will be more than happy to sit with you and tell you all about their life.
- Eat with a close friend or relative in a public place.
- Make eye contact when talking to others.
- Make an effort to greet others first or just say hello to strangers.
- Give people compliments.
- Go to a store and ask a clerk to help you find a product.
- Ask someone on the street for directions.

After coming up with a list of exposures that you will do, the next step to make an exposure hierarchy. This involves ranking each exposure you want to do on a scale of how hard you believe it will be to get through. Basically, what I did was rank my exposures on a least-feared to most-feared basis. This allows you to start out slow with the less-feared exposures, gain some confidence, and work your way up to more-feared situations. Doing baby steps is the key to making exposure therapy successful.

List Each Exposure You Would Like to Do: Hierarchy Rank

Now you can start doing some exposures. The way I would recommend you to start out is with imaginal exposures. This will get you ready for doing the real thing. First, start by finding a comfortable and quiet place you will not be interrupted or distracted. Next, start by doing some of your relaxation techniques that we have already gone through. Then, pick an item that you have in your exposure hierarchy that you have listed in the less-feared section. Close your eyes and imagine yourself entering the situation. Imagine what your surroundings look like, what kind of smells there are, what you hear, and things you can feel physically. Use all of your senses to make the situation in your head as real as you can make it. Next, imagine yourself going through that feared situation. You will probably get nervous or anxious, but use your relaxation techniques and coping statements to help you through it. Just keep in mind that the anxiety will go away and will not hurt you in any way. Sometimes before sitting down and doing an imaginal exposure, I will write out what will happen. You can even tape yourself with a tape recorder and record your thoughts or what you are feeling throughout the exposure. After you have practiced going through a feared event with imagination and become comfortable with the thought, you can move on to doing the real-life thing.

Taking on a feared social event in real life is a very big step at first. Keep in mind the great rewards you will gain from doing this: freedom from fear. Although you may feel anxious and very uncomfortable, going through the feared situations will not hurt you. Unlike in the imaginational exposure, you cannot always stage a real-life event when you want to. You may have to wait and play it by ear when a specific event that you would like to work on comes about. In general, the steps involved in carrying out real life exposures are similar to imaginal exposures. First, start out with challenge items that are low on your exposure hierarchy. Next, enter the feared situation and carry out the exposure. Your anxiety level will rise, but remember that this means the exposure is working. Allow yourself to feel the anxiety and realize it will not harm you. As you carry the same exposure out multiple times, your anxiety level should decrease each time you attempt it. When you do have anxiety, remember to use your breathing and relaxation techniques to manage your anxiety. If you get in a predicament in which you experience a great deal of anxiety in a certain situation, you can always back out and try doing an exposure that you feel is easier to get your confidence back. Before going back to the real life exposure that you backed out of, redo the imaginal process first. Remember to monitor your maladaptive thoughts that you may have throughout your exposures and construct alternative ways of thinking. Record all the exposures you do so you can keep track of them.

Reward yourself every time you successfully complete an exposure, whether you feel it went well or not. Remember that you are allowed to make mistakes. Many social phobics are perfectionists who do not deal well with making mistakes. Many of these individuals believe they will be judged the most negatively when making a mistake. You must learn to deal with the fact that you will make mistakes and that this does not automatically lead to disapproval. I will cover ways to deal with disapproval and rejection when they occur later in this chapter. But first, I would like to give you tips to follow in carrying out a successful exposure.

The first key into having a successful exposure is to go at your own pace. Diving into it too fast could actually be more harmful than helpful. Start with the most manageable situations, and then build your way up to the harder ones. Each exposure you do should be a confidence builder and give you a sense of accomplishment. You want to challenge yourself but not go so fast as to overwhelm yourself. In my own experience, I knew that I mastered a situation and could move on to another exposure when I felt I could repeat the exposure without difficulty. If you believe that you just barely squeaked through an exposure and had a significant amount of anxiety, I would suggest you repeat the exposure until you are comfortable with it.

The second tip to having a successful exposure is to minimize your distractions and be involved in every exposure. What I mean is that when you are carrying out an exposure; devote 100% of your energy to facing the task at hand instead of trying to distract yourself with outside surroundings in order to lessen your anxiety. For instance, pretend you have a fear of eating around coworkers. Say you are doing an exposure by going out to dinner with a friend. The whole time you might be looking at the people around you or concentrating on the decorations of the restaurant instead of the task you should be devoting your attention to. Remember to be using your coping skills you have learned and practice them when you are facing your fears so you can build confidence.

Another important lesson in having a successful exposure is to wait until your anxiety level drops before ending an exposure. If you end an exposure session early while you are still having significant anxiety, you will feel overwhelmed and will have little confidence in handling a similar situation in the future. If you give yourself time during an exposure to slowly drop your anxiety level, you reinforce in your mind that the specific fearful situation will not hurt you in the future and you can deal with the anxiety. Doing this repeatedly, will help you become less anxious and give you the confidence you need to be comfortable in a social atmosphere.

Next, practice exposures as often and as long as you can. If you allow too much time in between exposures, you can break the confidence you have while moving up your hierarchy ladder. Exposure after exposure helps you build more and more momentum in your quest to conquer your fears. If you break that chain, you may find yourself starting over at the very beginning in your exposure hierarchy and relearning your coping mechanisms.

Last, evaluate the progress you are making. Are you going at a reasonable pace? Do you feel like you are getting what you need out of each exposure? Can you feel your confidence building at all? How are your relaxation methods working? Do you need to make more coping statements for yourself? Ask yourself some general questions such as these to help you evaluate where you stand. Always keep reevaluating your goals. Maybe you are so far into your exposures and you feel you have even larger goals you would like to accomplish. Write these down and make a plan to help you successfully complete your goals.

Now comes the tricky part. While going through exposures, you are bound to run into disapproval and rejection from others. I know this terrifies you in many ways, but you are going to have to learn to deal with it and know that everyone in the world runs into the same predicaments. Rejection and disapproval is just a part of life. I am going to give you the best advice I can to help you through these times. Just know that you are going to have to deal with this sooner or later, and it is not the end of world by any means. It will make you stronger as a person and give you the confidence in dealing with future incidences.

Rejection at any point, weather it may be at first meeting or well into a relationship, can be painful and difficult for most of us. There are ways to prevent rejection from being an all out failure. Being turned down at any point in the process helps you to learn a little more about how to approach a stranger, have a conversation, make plans, go on a date, or move toward intimacy. If you learn something positive from the experience, you can bring that with you into your next experience. Without putting yourself in the position for possible rejection, you will never have the opportunity to obtain any meaningful social relationships.

Rejection can hurt, but it does not have to be devastating. It's perfectly normal to feel disappointed when you do not get the reaction you want. But all too often, people overemphasize the importance or meaning of rejection, especially when there are fairly superficial interactions taking place as with a first meeting or casual date. Here are some tips to keep rejection in perspective:

- Don't overthink or overanalyze the situation. Doing this will only increase your anxiety.
- Keep the feelings of disappointment specific to the rejection situation at hand.
- Try to keep it positive. Don't say, "No one ever wants to talk to me." Say, "Too bad the chemistry wasn't right for both of us."
- Try to learn some sort of lesson from your experience. Ask yourself what you might have done differently, if anything, but then move on.
- Don't beat yourself up about it.
- It is also nice to sit down with someone else and get another person's perspective on a specific situation. Also, just talking to a friend can take away a lot of disappointment you may be experiencing.

Giving presentations:

I would also like to give you tips for giving speeches in front of others. Public speaking is the most frequent form of circumscribed social phobia. Many may feel absolutely comfortable in social situations, but when it comes to making a presentation in front of others, they freeze up. These individuals may become so fearful of making presentations that they will do everything in their power to avoid it. Although you may not enjoy giving presentations, I will give you some tips to help deal with your anxieties.

First, you must prepare before you deliver your message in front of an audience. You must step back and think about who you will be delivering this speech to. Are they female or male? What is their age range? Are they educated about the topic material? Are they listening to your speech to further their knowledge base or are they required to listen to your speech for a school project? The more you know about your audience, the more you can prepare a speech that specifically targets them. Next, you need to find out what type of speech you need to prepare. Do you want to educate the audience? Do you want to convince them on a specific issue? Do you want to entertain them? You need to think about all of this before you actually start to prepare a speech.

The second thing you want to do when preparing a speech is to give yourself a few weeks ahead of time to begin. Don't write a speech a couple days before you must deliver it, because it will only give you more anxiety than you would normally have. Next, instead of sitting and trying to write your speech from beginning to end, allow yourself time to brainstorm. What points do you want to be sure to deliver to your audience? After brainstorming what ideas you wish to convey to your audience, write down a quick outline, starting with the most important points you will talk about. From this, write some smaller points you would like to add to each main topic. Write down your outline on note cards and don't write full sentences out. The meaning of this is not to get caught up in remembering exactly every word you want to say in your speech but to make sure you hit home on the most important topics.

Prepare an opening statement to draw the attention of your audience. The first sentence should sum up what you will be trying to get across, what the topic material will be, and your key points. In your opening statement, you want to grab your audience's attention and give them a reason to want to hear what you have to say next. The opening statement is something you want to write down word for word and really practice it. Show the audience that you are excited about delivering the information to them. If you are interested in the material and excited, your audience will be more likely to do the same. Memorize your opening statement so you can express your emotions during your delivery instead of worrying about remembering what to say. Try to use simple language in your speech. Don't use big words just to try and impress your audience.

Practice, practice, practice! After preparing your speech, you need to practice it and time it. Practice your speech several times on your own. After getting down what you want to say, do some imaginal work before giving it to a live audience. Sit down and imagine yourself actually giving the speech in front of others. Use your relaxation techniques to control your anxiety. Ask some friends and family members to sit down and listen to you give your speech. Have them give you feedback afterward to what you could improve on. The more you practice your speech, the more confident you will be in delivering it.

So, it's now the day to give your presentation, and you are nervous. It's okay. Even people who get in front of an audience and talk every day get a little anxious. The key is to use your anxiety as a positive force. Instead of using that boost of adrenaline for fear, transform it into excitement. When delivering your speech, use some strong hand gestures and facial expressions to get rid of that extra excitement you have. Make sure you make strong eye contact with your audience. Just pick out someone in the audience that has a friendly face if you don't know anyone and focus on that person for a few seconds. Be confident and show everyone how excited you are about the material you are giving them. Usually if you show excitement and enthusiasm, the audience will respond in a positive way. Sometimes it is good to get the audience involved and give them visual aids. At times it may be appropriate to ask someone his or her opinion. Make sure that at the end of your presentation you ask your audience if they have any questions. Do your best to answer their question as completely as possible, and if you don't know the answer, don't make one up. If you don't know an answer to a question, just tell that individual that you will do some research on it and will provide him or her with the information as soon as possible.

Remember that public speaking is a skill that is developed. The more experience and practice you have, the better you will get. Do not try to be perfect while making a speech, but try to connect with the audience!

Chapter 8:

Learning basic social skills

If you are like many with SAD, you have spent a lot of time avoiding social situations and may not have much experience in interacting with others. If this is the case for you, you may need to relearn or improve your social skills. First, sit back and think about how you interact with others. Do you have trouble starting or maintaining conversations? How is your body language when communicating with others? Do you make eye contact? These are just a few questions you should be asking yourself. You may need a lot of work on your social skills or just a little. No matter what, I believe that if you just read over this chapter and practice some of the skills you lack, you could become a better communicator altogether.

I remember when I was preparing for interviews to get into physician assistant school. I had to sit in front of interviewers I did not know and somehow sway them to choose me to be part of their program. I had to be outgoing and likable. For someone with social anxiety disorder, this is very hard to do and was totally nerve-wracking. I did everything to prepare myself for these interviews. I would read article after article on communication and the ability of getting your point across to others. To my surprise, communication involves way more than just the words you have to say. Only around 7% of the message people receive from you actually comes from the words you say to them. Your tone of voice accounts for around 38% of the impression you make on someone. The most influential type of communication that affects one's impression of you comes from the nonverbal cues you give off (55%). Nonverbal communication includes how you look at someone, your posture, eye contact, and so on. This was shocking to me at first, but made sense after I thought about it. Have you ever talked to someone that had an angry face and was trying to be nice to you? No matter what they said to you, you somehow didn't believe what they were saying or got the impression that maybe they were just being insincere. Social skills are key to making friendships, getting what you want, and becoming likable.

I will begin by describing nonverbal communication and give you some basic skills that you can practice in real life, just like exposures. You can continually add these skills together as you learn them.

Although many people say they look on the inside to judge a person, rather than on the outside (physical appearance), your outside appearance is the first impression someone gets of you. Although it seems superficial to tell you to keep up your looks, it is very important. Your grooming habits and the way you dress also give off information on the way you take care of yourself. You don't have to keep up with the newest fashions and dress, but just be aware of what type of image you are projecting to others. Be comfortable with the type of style you choose, and have confidence in yourself.

Another key component of nonverbal communication is body language. Your body language tells others how you are feeling, even before talking to them. It gives people an idea of how receptive you are to communicating with them. For example, the way you stand at a social event sends a message to others. If you are standing with others, socializing, and smiling, then you are more likely to become approached. If you are off on your own in the corner and standing with your arms crossed, you are giving off a less-inviting impression. You must learn to project a friendly, open image in order to develop effective body language. Another, more challenging skill, is learning to read another person's nonverbal behavioral signals before approaching him or her. Posture has a lot to do with a person's body language. A closed posture, which includes sitting with arms or legs crossed, or a hand over your mouth while talking, gives the signal that you are not interested in talking with another person. Standing with your arms crossed gives off a signal that you are displeased or you are defensive. An open posture includes having your arms relaxed, not crossed, and your hands away from your mouth. An open posture tells others that you are friendly, approachable, and willing to have a conversation. Also, your body orientation is very important, along with your posture. If your body is directly facing someone, this shows the other person you are interested in them. If you have your body turned away from another or even angled away from them, then this shows you are trying to avoid them.

Another important detail that you may want to pay attention to is personal space. Personal space refers to the area immediately around your body. Generally, people with SAD are more likely to stand too far away when conversing with others. Standing too far away from a person when talking, may signal to him or her that you are not interested. Personal distance usually ranges from 1.5 to 4 feet when talking with friends. Social distances, which are usually taken with impersonal acquaintances, range from 4 to 12 feet. Just pay attention how far you stand away when conversing with others.

Eye contact is a key aspect to remember when communicating. Eyes tell a lot about what a person is feeling and his or her immediate reactions. Frequent eye contact in general is a sign for approval, interest, or affection. Those with SAD are more likely to have too little eye contact. This can signal to others that you are disinterested or that you don't want to give them the time of day. Sometimes I catch myself totally disinterested in what someone is saying to me, but if I look him or her straight in the eyes, lean forward, and shake my head in approval, that gives the other person a feeling that I care about what he or she is saying to me. It is a lot of what you signal to another person nonverbally that sparks his or her attention.

Last, remember to be aware of your facial expressions. Your face is the gateway to how you feel. If you are smiling, others think you are in a good mood and are more likely to interact. Likewise, if you are frowning all the time, people are less likely to approach you. Many of the nonverbal cues you give off may be unconscious. You must become aware of these cues and learn to change your habits in order to become more likable.

Now, let's concentrate on your verbal communication skills. I will start by focusing on the art of conversation. It takes a lot of practice and confidence to become comfortable just striking up a conversation with someone you may not know. With having SAD, this will be very intimidating to you. Again, it is all about practicing and getting more experience. The first thing to do in striking up a conversation is to introduce yourself. You want to first greet a person with a smile, say hello, and tell them your name. At the same time, you can shake the person's hand while greeting him or her. This may be straight forward, but I have seen people greet others with their hands in their pockets. Keeping your hands in your pockets shows that you are not very inviting or interested in talking to the person. When shaking a person's hand, make sure you have a decent grip. Don't shake someone's hand like a wet piece of spaghetti, and don't try to grip their hand so hard you break it. Just use a firm and confident hand shake.

After introducing themselves, many people make what is known as small talk. A lot of people think that small talk is just meaningless babble. In actuality, small talk allows you to communicate nonverbally with another person and helps you find out something you may have in common. If you and the person you are interacting with are both giving off nonverbal cues that show you are both open and willing to have a more in-depth conversation, you can move on to a more meaningful talk.

Having a conversation with someone entails taking an active role in moving a conversation along. All too many times, people with SAD depend on others to maintain and move the conversation forward, which puts the other person in a vulnerable position. It is key to learn strategies for keeping a conversation alive and flowing.

The first rule in keeping a conversation going is by asking questions. There are two types of questions you need to be aware of: open-ended questions and closed questions. Closed questions are those questions that you can answer with a simple answer and do nothing to move a conversation forward. For example, you can ask someone if they enjoy their job. That person could answer a simple yes or no to that question. On the other hand, open-ended questions are more general questions that require the other person to explain themselves and elaborate on their answer. For example, you could have asked that same person what their job duties entail and what they enjoy or dislike about each duty. Open-ended questions cause the other person to elaborate and show that you are interested in what they have to say. In general, people love to talk about themselves, especially when the listener is showing interest in what they are saying.

Another way you can keep a conversation moving is by being a good listener. This may seem easy, but for many people with SAD it is not. People with social phobia have a hard time listening because they are always having internal thoughts about themselves. They are worried about how they look or weather they are sweating, and so on. You must concentrate on what the communicator is saying and pay close attention. If you don't, then that person may think you are disinterested in what he or she is saying and may end the conversation. A useful tool in showing your interest is paraphrasing what the other person said to you. Don't just repeat what the person said, but put it in different words, and this will show him or her that they have your attention. You can even ask the person further questions when he or she answers you back. Being a great listener takes time and lots of practice. Practice your listening techniques with your friends and start being more observant with conversations around you.

Self-disclosure is yet another skill to master and put into use while communicating with others. This entails sharing your thoughts and feelings while having a conversation. If you don't disclose anything about yourself or your views on topics, then people may mistake this in a negative light. They may think you don't care about the topic or that you don't wish to continue talking to them. Let the person you are talking to get to know the real you. Try to stay up to date on current events and have some conversation topics ready, so when you are ready to give your opinion, you will be a bit more prepared.

Another important social skill is that of giving and receiving compliments. Sometimes a compliment is even a good way to get a conversation started. Try to be specific with your compliment instead of general, and it will be more meaningful. For example you could say, "I like what you are wearing today," and that would be a somewhat general comment. It would be more meaningful if you said something like, "I love your shirt and how it matches your eye color." If someone gives you a complement, make sure you acknowledge it. Look at the person and thank him or her. You can even tell the person that you are appreciative that he or she took the time to notice.

Most of the tips above can be practiced in many situations. Practice your body language, facial expressions, and listening skills initially in environments where you are already comfortable. After you get practice, you can proceed to interacting with new people you meet. The ultimate goal is for you to become more comfortable in social situations. The more comfortable you get with your social skills, the more self-confidence you will build. Remember this process will take time and effort on your part. Be patient, and soon you will be that person you have always wanted to be!

Chapter 9:

Is there differences in the effectiveness between psychotherapy treatment and drug therapy? A summary of the most up-to-date research.

So I added this chapter to the book for those who are curious if there is a difference between medication and psychotherapy in treating SAD. I also had a strong interest in this subject matter while in school. I wrote my master's thesis on this topic, so I have researched this in great detail. In reality, there have been only a handful of studies that have actually compared psychotherapy to drug therapy head-to-head. There are many more studies going on currently, and research is only in the beginning stages. All we can do right now is compare the current study results and give some basic generalizations and theories. This chapter is technical in its descriptions, and you may want to skip it if it does not interest you. At the end of this chapter I give an overview of the material covered in this chapter. If you don't want to read all of the details of the following studies, you can skip to the end of the chapter to get an overview of the material covered.

Few studies have directly compared pharmacological and cognitive behavioral treatments for social phobia. Results of two previous studies showed better outcomes with cognitive behavioral treatments than drug therapy. However, the medications studied were buspirone and atenolol, neither of which surpassed the efficacy of a placebo, limiting the value of the study. Currently, there have been only three studies that directly compared CBT and effective drug therapies.

The first true study directly comparing an effective drug therapy to CBT (an effective psychotherapy) in SAD patients was from Heimburg et al. (1998), comparing phenalzine directly with cognitive-behavioral group therapy. One hundred thirty-three (133) patients participated in this study and received 12 weeks of CBGT, phenelzine therapy, pill placebo administration, or educational-supportive (ES) group therapy (an attention–placebo treatment of equal credibility to CBGT). Pre- and posttreatment assessment included an independent assessor interview, self-report questionnaires, and a behavioral test. Groups of five to seven patients were then randomly assigned to 12 weekly sessions of one of the four treatment groups, as described above. Phenelzine and double-blind pill placebo were administered by a psychiatrist, and CBGT and ES were conducted by a psychologist. Assessments were repeated after 6 (interview and questionnaires only) and 12 weeks of treatment.

Results from this study showed that both phenelzine therapy and CBGT were effective in treating social phobia. Compared with pill placebo and attention-placebo conditions, both were associated with higher rates of response after 12 weeks. Results showed that 77% of patients receiving phenelzine and 75% of patients undergoing CBGT who completed treatment (65% and 58% of enrolled patients, respectively) were classified as responders, significantly more than for placebo drug use or ES group therapy. Patients receiving phenelzine were also less anxious than control patients on most IA (independent assessor), self-report, and behavior test measures. Cognitive behavioral group therapy surpassed one or both control conditions on many of these measures as well. Although rates of response to phenelzine therapy and CBGT were similar, after 12 weeks, the pattern of response was different. Fifty-two percent of patients taking phenelzine but only 28% of patients undergoing CBGT were classified as responders after 6 weeks. Expressed otherwise, 80% of 12-week phenelzine responders reached that threshold after 6 weeks, whereas only 48% of 12-week CBGT responders did so. On several IA ratings, patients receiving phenelzine were rated as less anxious than patients in the other conditions after 6 weeks. On most ratings, patients undergoing CBGT were rated as less anxious than patients receiving ES, but were rated as less anxious than patients taking placebo on only one midtreatment measure. After 12 weeks, the superiority of CBGT to the control conditions was greater. Because CBGT was characterized by an increased rate of response between midtreatment and posttreatment, it is unclear whether patients receiving CBGT had achieved the maximum benefit after 12 weeks. An extended period of intensive treatment may benefit CBGT efficacy.

There were limitations in the Heimburg et al. (1998) study. First, there were no weekly assessments of patient status. To do so would have provided a more in-depth analysis of patient progress and made the data more amenable to other statistical approaches (e.g., survival analysis). Second, there were no measurements of patient disability, functional impairment, or lowered life satisfaction. These types of data are increasingly recognized as important and have been related to outcome of treatment of social phobia. Furthermore, this study was unable to examine outcomes of other disorders that may have been comorbid with patients' social phobia. Things to consider are that the study focused on outcomes during the first 12 weeks of the study comparing phenelzine therapy and CBGT. However, the treatments may have different effects over time, and subsets of patients (e.g., patients with generalized vs. nongeneralized social phobia) may have more or less unique patterns of response to the treatments.

The second study I want to present to you was the first study that had patients combine CBT and a SSRI together. The Blomhoff study primarily compared the efficacy of treatment with sertraline (Zoloft) or placebo in a controlled, double-blind, randomized design in primary care patients with generalized social phobia. In addition, primary care physicians were trained in a brief exposure therapy program with an added practical, short-term behavioral treatment intervention. The study also examined the efficacy of this brief exposure treatment performed by primary care physicians, as well as the efficacy of combined sertraline and exposure therapy. Patients ($n = 387$) received sertraline 50-150 mg or placebo for 24 weeks. Patients were additionally randomly selected to undergo exposure therapy or general medical care. The patients were defined as responders, partial responders, or nonresponders based on assessments on the investigator-rated Clinical Global Impression–Social Phobia scale (CGI–SP) and the patient-rated SPS. Investigators made intermediate efficacy ratings after 4, 8, 12, and 16 weeks, and final efficacy assessment after 24 weeks of treatment. Response was defined as a reduction of at least 50% on SPS-assessed symptom burden compared with baseline, a CGI–SP overall severity score at the final visit in the *no mental illness* to *mild severity* range (≤ 3), and a CGI–SP overall improvement score of very much or much improved (≤ 2). Nonresponse was defined as less than 25% reduction on SPS compared with baseline, or CGI–SP overall improvement rating of no change or worse (≥ 4). Partial response was defined as all responses between the criteria for response and nonresponse.

This is a brief discussion of the exposure therapy that was given in this study. In the first session, patients were informed of the rationale for treatment, and the main problem areas were identified. In the next session agreement was made about homework assignments, and the use of a symptom monitoring diary during exposure training was explained. In the remaining sessions, the patients were instructed to gradually expose themselves to feared situations, and thus learn new coping strategies. They were told to stay as long as they could in the phobic situation, ideally until their anxiety decreased. All patients received homework assignments between the sessions and brought a report of the training with them to the next session. The physician helped the patients to identify goals, learn new coping strategies, and try out self-exposure training.

The Blomhoff study showed that sertraline-treated patients were significantly more improved than non-sertraline-treated patients ($x^2 = 12.53$, $P < 0.001$; odds ratio = 0.534; 95% Cl 0.347-0.835). No significant difference was observed between exposure and non-exposure-treated patients ($x^2 = 2.18$, $P = 0.140$; odds ratio = 0.732; 95% Cl 0.475-1.134). In the pairwise comparisons, combined sertraline and exposure ($x^2 = 12.32$; $P < 0.001$) and sertraline ($x^2 = 10.13$; $P = 0.002$) were significantly superior to placebo.

The results of this study demonstrated that sertraline, both alone and combined with exposure therapy, are effective and well tolerated in the treatment of generalized social phobia carried out in primary care. The study suggested an enhanced efficacy of combined sertraline and exposure treatment, primarily through increasing the number of patients who achieved response. There were no statistical interaction between sertraline and exposure therapy, this finding most probably must be interpreted as the result of additive treatment effects. Sertraline/CBT and sertraline alone, but not CBT/PBO, exceeded the response from PBO alone.

The most recent study published (Davidson et. al., year) compared an SSRI with CCBT. This study, like the previous study combining Zoloft with exposure therapy, is the second to give a combination of both CCBT and an SSRI. This study however used fluoxetine (Prozac) for the drug of choice in treatment and group CBT. The following study had five overall goals to compare the effects of 14 weeks of treatment (a) with fluoxetine (FLU) alone, (b) with group alone (CCBT), (c) with combined CCBT/FLU, (d) with CCBT/placebo (PBO; to take into account nonspecific pill taking), and (e) with PBO alone. This study was a randomized, double-blind, and placebo-controlled trial. Subjects meeting a primary diagnosis of generalized social phobia were recruited via advertisement. Seven hundred twenty-two were screened, and 295 were randomized and available for inclusion in an intention-to-treat efficacy analysis. Treatment lasted for 14 weeks. Fluoxetine and PBO were administered at doses from 10 mg/d to 60 mg/d (or equivalent). Group comprehensive cognitive behavioral therapy was administered weekly for 14 sessions. An independent, blinded evaluator assessed response with the Brief Social Phobia Scale (BSPS) and Clinical Global Impressions (CGI) scales as primary outcomes. A videotaped behavioral assessment served as a secondary outcome, using the Subjective Units of Distress Scale. Adverse effects were measured by self-rating.

This study found the following results: Clinical Global Impressions scale response rates in the intention-to-treat sample were 29 (50.9%; FLU), 31 (51.7%; CCBT), 32 (54.2%; CCBT/FLU), 30 (50.8%; CCBT/PBO), and 19 (31.7%; PBO). All treatments were found as being significantly better than PBO. On the Brief Social Phobia Scale, all active treatments were superior to PBO. In the linear mixed-effects models analysis, FLU was more effective than CCBT/FLU, CCBT/PBO, and PBO at Week 4; CCBT was also more effective than CCBT/FLU and CCBT/PBO. By the final visit, all active treatments were superior to PBO but did not differ from each other. In adults with generalized social phobia (GSP), this study demonstrated efficacy for FLU and CCBT relative to PBO, but no evidence for greater benefit of combined treatment over monotherapies.

Conclusions of the three studies and comparisons:

Comparing the results of the fluoxetine and group CBT study(Davidson et al. year) with the study of phenelzine and group CBT by Heimberg et al (1998), indicates that the two studies have similar PBO response rates (31% and 33%, respectively) and broadly comparable rates of response to group therapy (52% and 58%, respectively). Response rates to FLU and phenelzine were 51% and 65%, respectively. Given a very broad spectrum of activity for monoamine oxidase inhibitors, it is conceivable that phenelzine carries greater benefit than an SSRI, a hypothesis consistent with a recent meta-analysis by Hidalgo et al. (2001). However, in previous studies, fluoxetine has failed to show a significant difference from placebo. Therefore, Prozac may possibly not be the most appropriate SSRI to study for the treatment of generalized social phobia (GSP).

In the Blomhoff et al, (year) study, again Sertraline/CBT and sertraline alone, but not CBT/PBO, exceeded the response from PBO alone. Combined sertraline/CBT tended to produce greater benefits. However, on 28-week posttreatment follow-up, initial CBT alone was associated with further gain, whereas sertraline alone or combined with CBT was associated with deterioration. This study differed from the other two studies in sample characteristics, type of CBT, and lack of a CBT-alone group, which may account for some of the different findings. In the Davidson et al. (year) study, combining FLU with CCBT did not provide any greater therapeutic benefit. One possible contributing reason may be the distracting physical complaints that arise early with medication and may be a reason for sequential treatment rather than simultaneous initiation.

The Davidson et al. (year) study used a 2-level approach (piecewise linear growth model) and found FLU generated a faster response than the other treatments; at Week 4, FLU showed superiority to CCBT/FLU, CCBT/PBO, and PBO. However, the degree of change at posttreatment did not differ between FLU and CCBT. Thus, these findings are similar to Heimberg et al, (1998) who reported an earlier advantage for phenelzine over CBT, with the two treatments being comparable by Week 12. Such a finding suggests that greater advantage would accrue from a strategy of initial treatment with an SSRI, followed by augmentation with psychosocial treatment after 4 to 8 weeks of drug therapy.

Future Studies:

With only three studies comparing the effectiveness of drug and psychotherapy, only general theories can be made from these results. There is much more research that is needed to be done with respect to treatment of social anxiety disorder. There have not been studies comparing SSRIs head-to-head in the treatment of GSP so it is hard to tell what medication, if any, is more favorable to use in comparison studies with psychotherapy. Furthermore, recent evidence suggests that individual CBT produces better results than group CBT in GSP. In terms of designs for future research, there should first be studies that directly compare drug therapy, such as SSRIs, to see if there are significant differences in effectiveness. Second, because there have been some findings to how effective individual CBT is to group CBT, there should be studies conducted that match these two forms of psychotherapy to find the most efficacious. Last, after finding the most beneficial drug therapy and psychotherapy in treating SAD, there should be some large group studies conducted that directly compare these different types of therapies head to head. Another aspect that should be added to these future studies is to have some long-term studies that do compare the duration of effectiveness of medication versus psychotherapy, to see if there are any significant differences in effectiveness in the long run or significantly different relapse rates.

With respect to whether these three current research studies have altered future treatment of SAD in clinical practice, I don't believe it has. Currently, many physicians and psychiatrists first attempt drug therapy in treating social phobia so that patients have relatively quick resolution of their symptoms. Also, in a lot of rural settings, there isn't the availability of a therapist to administer CBT.

Conclusion:

I truly hope that this book has helped you in some way. I believe that SAD is probably the most common psychiatric disorder that few are aware of. I want to put an end to that and educate everyone on how very important this disorder is. SAD can be very devastating and make people with the disorder miserable in their everyday lives. if not treated. Please spread the word about SAD and even pass this book along to someone you may feel might be in need.

Please make sure to visit your family doctor and talk with him or her about your symptoms. You must have a professional accurately diagnose you first. Your family doctor will also prescribe medicine to you or refer you to a specialist who deals with SAD on a day-to-day basis. Counseling is also important, and many health care professionals such as your family doctor can help point you in the right direction. Please get the help you need and fight this ugly disorder. I promise that the hard work will all be worth it to you in the end. Thank you for your support and God bless you.

Scientific Bibliography

The following selection of references and scientific articles on the subject of social anxiety disorder were used in preparing this book:

Agras, W.S., & Clark, D.B. (1991). The assessment and treatment of performance anxiety in musicians. *Am Journal of Psychiatry,148*, 598–605.

American Psychiatric Association (1994). *Diagnostic and statistical manual of mental disorders* (4th ed.). Washington, DC: Author.

Barnett, S. D., Davidson, J..R. T., & Hidalgo, R. B. (2001). Social anxiety disorder in review: two decades of progress. *International Journal of Neuropsychopharmacology., 4*, 279–298.

Becker, R. E., Dodge, C. S., Heimberg, R. G., Hope, D. A., Kennedy, C. R., & Zollo, L. (1990). Cognitive behavioral group treatment of social phobia: Comparison with a credible placebo control. *Cogn Ther Res., 14*:1–23.

Becker, R. E., Goldfinger, K., Heimberg, R. G., & Vermilyea, J. A. (1985). Treatment of social phobia by exposure, cognitive restructuring, and homework assignments. *J Nerv Ment Dis., 173*, 236–245.

Beidel, D. C., Jacob, R., & Turner, S. M. (1994). Social phobia: A comparison of behavior therapy and atenolol. *J Consult Clin Psychol., 62*, 350–358.

Blendell, K.. Heimberg, R. G. , Holt, C. S., & Salzman, D. (1993). Cognitive behavioral group treatment of social phobia: effectiveness at 5-year follow-up. *Cogn Ther Res., 17*,325–339.

Brown, E. J., Heimberg, R. G., & Juster, H. R. (1995). Social phobia subtype and avoidant personality disorder: Effect on severity of social phobia, impairment, and outcome of cognitive-behavioral treatment. *Behav Ther., 26*,467–486.

Bruce, T. J., & Sy Atezaz Saeed. (1999). Social Anxiety Disorder: A common, underrecognized mental disorder. *American Family Physician., 60*(8).

Bruch, M. A., Heimberg, R. G., & Hope, D. A. (1995). Dismantling cognitive-behavioral group therapy for social phobia. *Behav Res Ther., 33*, 637–650.

Bruch, M. A., Heimberg, R. G. , & Hope, D. A. (1991). States of mind model and cognitive change in treated social phobics. *Cogn Ther Res., 15*,429–441.

Blomhoff, S. (2001). Randomised controlled general practice trial of sertraline, exposure therapy and combined treatment in generalised social phobia. *The British Journal of Psychiatry, 179*, 23-30.

Chambless, D. L., & Edelman, R. (1995). Adherence during sessions and homework in cognitive-behavioral group treatment of social phobia. *Behav Res Ther., 33*,573–577.

Clark, D. M., Heidenreich, T., Lauterbach, W., Peitz, M., & Stangier, U. (2003). Cognitive therapy for social phobia: Individual versus group treatment. *Behav Res Ther., 41*, 991–1007.

Coles, M. E., Eng, W., Heimberg, R. G., & Safren, S. A. (2001). *Quality of life in social anxiety disorder: Diagnosis, assessment and treatment*. New York, NY: Guilford Press.

Davidson, J. (2004). Fluoxetine, comprehensive cognitive behavioral therapy, and placebo in generalized social phobia. *Arch Gen Psychiatry., 61*,1005–1013.

Haug, T. T., Hellstrøm, K., Blomhoff, S., Humble, M., Madsbu, H-P. & Wold, J. E. (2000). The   treatment of social phobia in general practice. Is exposure therapy feasible? *Family Practice, 17*, 114–118.

Heimberg, R. G. (1993). Specific issues in the cognitive-behavioral treatment of social phobia. *J Clin Psychiatry, 54*(12), 36–45.

Heimberg, R. G., Hope, D. A., Liebowitz, M.R., & Schneier, F. R. (1998). Cognitive behavioral group therapy vs phenelzine therapy for social phobia 12-week outcome. *Arch Gen Psychiatry, 55*,1133–1141.

Heimberg, R. G., & Juster, H. R. (1995). Cognitive behavioral treatment: Literature review. In R. Heimberg, M. Liebowitz, D.

Hope, & F. Schneier (Eds.), *Social phobia: Diagnosis, assessment and treatment* (pp. 261–309). New York, NY: Guilford Press.

Heimberg, R.G., & Leung, A.W. (1996). Homework compliance, perceptions of control, and outcome of cognitive-behavioral treatment of social phobia. *Behav Res Ther., 34*, 423–432.

Henning, C. (2006). *Intensive exposure therapy.* Retrieved from http://panicdisorder.about.com/ od/exposuretherapy/

Hofmann, S. G. (2001). *Cognitive mediation of treatment Change in social phobia.*
Part of these results were presented at the NIMH workshop Psychotherapeutic Interventions: How and Why They Work.

Herbert, J.D., Hope, D.A., & White, C. (1995). Diagnostic subtype, avoidant personality disorder, and efficacy of cognitive-behavioral group therapy for social phobia. *Cogn Ther Res., 19*, 399–417.

Jacobson, J. L. (2001). *Psychiatric Secrets* (2nd ed.). Willow Grove, PA: Hanley and Belfus.

Lehne, R. A. (2004). *Pharmacology for nursing care.* Lehne, MO: Saunders.

Moore, D. P. & Jefferson, J. W. (2004). *Handbook of Medical Psychiatry.* Philadelphia, PA: Mosby..

Pollack, M. H. (2001). Comorbidity, neurobiology, and pharmacotherapy of social anxiety disorder. *Journal of Clinical Psychiatry, 62*(12), 24–29.

CPSIA information can be obtained at www.ICGtesting.com
Printed in the USA
LVOW132028090712

289404LV00002B/1/P